Colorful TUNISIAN AFGHANS to Crochet

GLENDA WINKLEMAN

Contents

3 Hope Rose Afghan

8 Summer Blues Afghan

13 Victorian Rose Afghan

16 Pennsylvania Dutch Afghan

21 Farmhouse Afghan

24 Spring Butterfly Afghan

30 Stitch Guide

31 Metric Conversion Charts

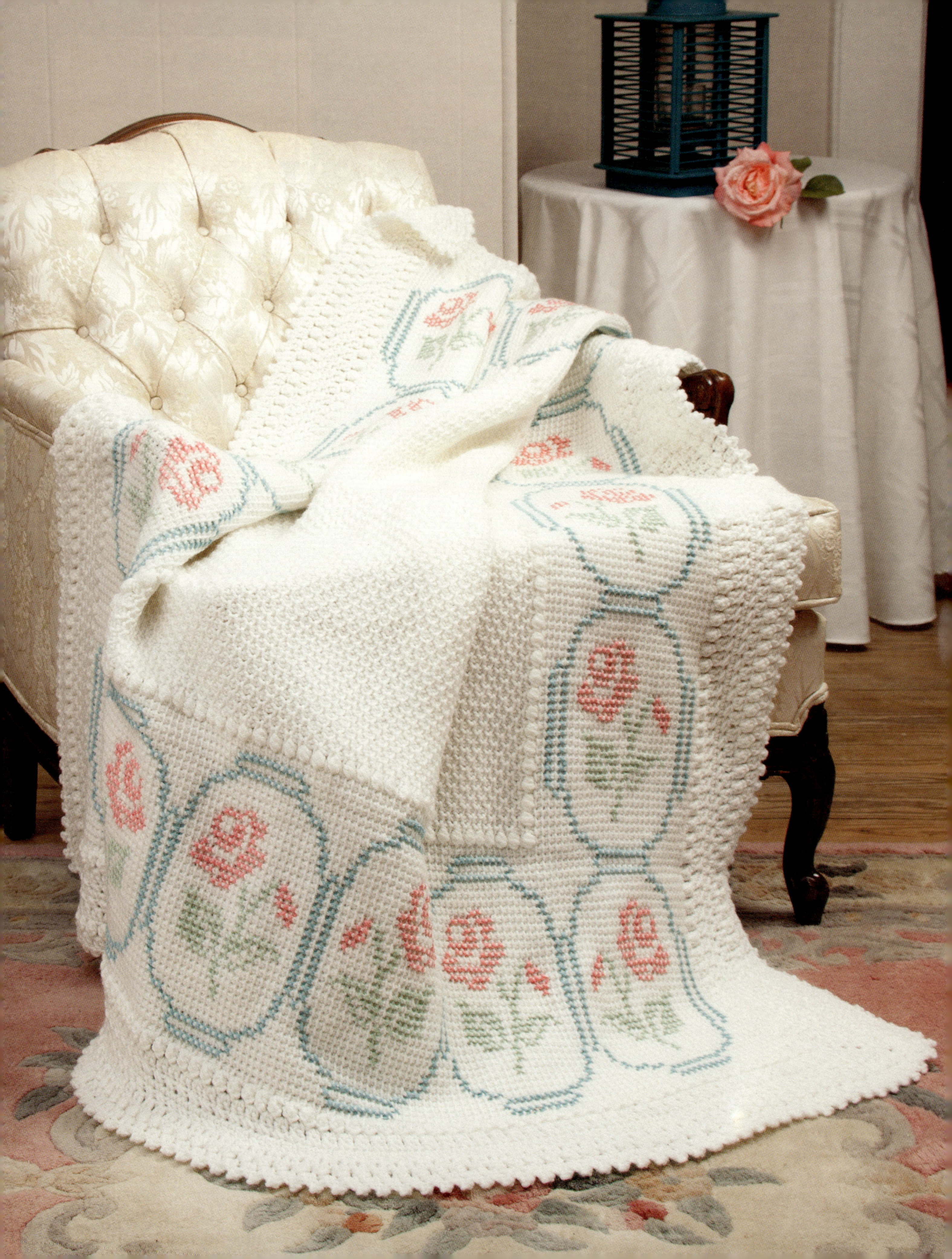

HOPE ROSE *Afghan*

SKILL LEVEL
■ ■ ☐ ☐
EASY

FINISHED MEASUREMENTS
50 inches wide x 59½ inches long

MATERIALS
- Red Heart Super Saver medium (worsted) weight acrylic yarn (7 oz/364 yds/198g per skein):
   8 skeins #316 soft white
   1 skein each #505 Aruba sea, #668 honeydew and #706 perfect pink
- Size K/10½/6.5mm afghan crochet hook or size needed to obtain gauge
- Size I/9/5.5mm crochet hook
- Tapestry needle

GAUGE
With afghan hook: 15 sts and 13 rows = 4 inches

PATTERN NOTES
Weave in ends as work progresses.

Join with slip stitch as indicated unless otherwise stated.

Chain-3 at beginning of round counts as first double crochet unless otherwise stated.

SPECIAL STITCHES
Bobble: Hold yarn to back of hook, insert hook in vertical st indicated, yo, pull yarn through st, keeping lp on hook, [yo, insert hook in same vertical st, pull yarn through st] twice *(5 lps on hook)*, yo, pull yarn through all 5 lps on hook.

Popcorn (pc): 3 dc in indicated st, drop lp from hook, insert hook from front to back under top 2 lps of first dc, pick up dropped lp and pull it through st, ch 1 to secure.

Crossed single crochet (crossed sc): Sk next st, sc in next st, working backward, sc in previously sk st.

Picot: Ch 3, sl st in last st made.

AFGHAN
CENTER
Row 1: With afghan hook and soft white, ch 151, working from right to left, insert hook in 2nd ch from hook, yo, draw through ch, *insert hook in next ch, yo, draw through ch, rep from * across keeping all lps on hook *(151 lps on hook)*, yo, draw through 1 lp on hook, **yo, draw through 2 lps on hook, rep from ** across until 1 lp rem on hook.

Rows 2–38: Working from right to left, insert hook in 2nd vertical st from hook, yo, draw yarn through st, *insert hook in next vertical st, yo, draw yarn through st, rep from * across keeping all lps on hook *(151 lps on hook)*, **2nd half of row:** yo, draw yarn through 1 lp on hook, **yo, draw yarn through 2 lps on hook, rep from ** across until 1 lp rem on hook *(counts as first lp of next row)*.

Note: *Rem instructions are written for first half of rows only, all sts are worked in vertical sts across. Rep 2nd half of row on each row throughout. Top of each bobble counts as next vertical st.*

Row 39: Working from right to left, insert hook in 2nd vertical st from hook, yo, draw yarn through st, [insert hook in next vertical st, yo, draw yarn through st] 29 times, **bobble** *(see Special Stitches)* in next st, [insert hook in next vertical st, yo, draw yarn through st, bobble in next st] 44 times, [insert hook in next vertical st, yo, draw yarn through st] 31 times. *(151 lps on hook)*

Row 40: Working from right to left, insert hook in 2nd vertical st from hook, yo, draw yarn through st, [insert hook in next vertical st, yo,

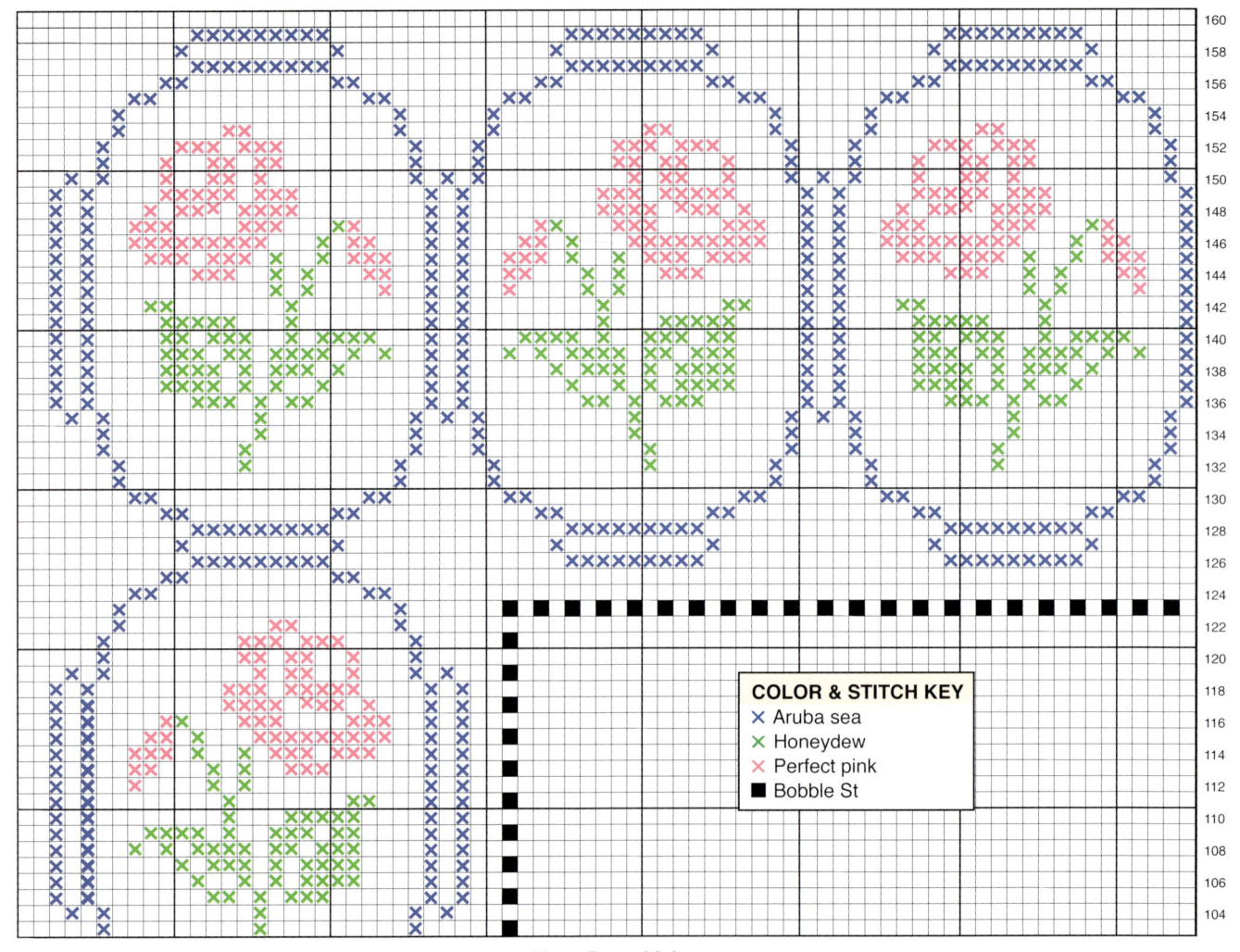

Hope Rose Afghan
Top Left Chart

COLOR & STITCH KEY
× Aruba sea
× Honeydew
× Perfect pink
■ Bobble St

draw yarn through st] 30 times, with yarn in front of hook, insert hook in next vertical st, yo, draw yarn through st, [with yarn in back of hook, insert hook in next vertical st, yo, draw yarn through st, with yarn in front of hook, insert hook in next vertical st, yo, draw yarn through st] 43 times, [insert hook in next vertical st, yo, draw yarn through st] 32 times. *(151 lps on hook)*

Row 41: Working from right to left, insert hook in 2nd vertical st from hook, yo, draw yarn through st, [insert hook in next vertical st, yo, draw yarn through st] 29 times, bobble in next st, with yarn in back of hook, insert hook in next vertical st, yo, draw yarn through st, [with yarn in front of hook, insert hook in next vertical st, yo, draw yarn through st, with yarn in back of hook, insert hook in next vertical st, yo, draw yarn through st] 43 times, bobble in next st, [insert hook in next vertical st, yo, draw yarn through st] 31 times. *(151 lps on hook)*

Rows 42–123: [Rep rows 40 and 41 alternately] 41 times.

Row 124: Rep row 39.

Rows 125–160: Rep row 2.

Row 161: Sl st in each vertical st across. Fasten off.

EMBROIDERY
With RS facing and using **cross-stitches** *(see illustration)*, follow chart to cross-stitch design on Center.

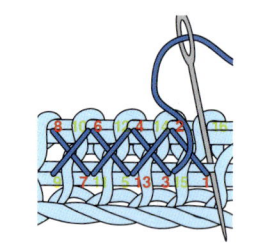

Note: *Make sure to count row-end st as a st when counting to start design.*

Cross-Stitch over Afghan Stitch

BORDER
Rnd 1: With RS facing and 1 short end at top and with size I hook, **join** *(see Pattern Notes)* soft white in top right-hand corner st, **pc** *(see Special Stitches)* in corner st, [ch 1, sk next st, pc in next st] across to last st before next corner, ch 1, pc

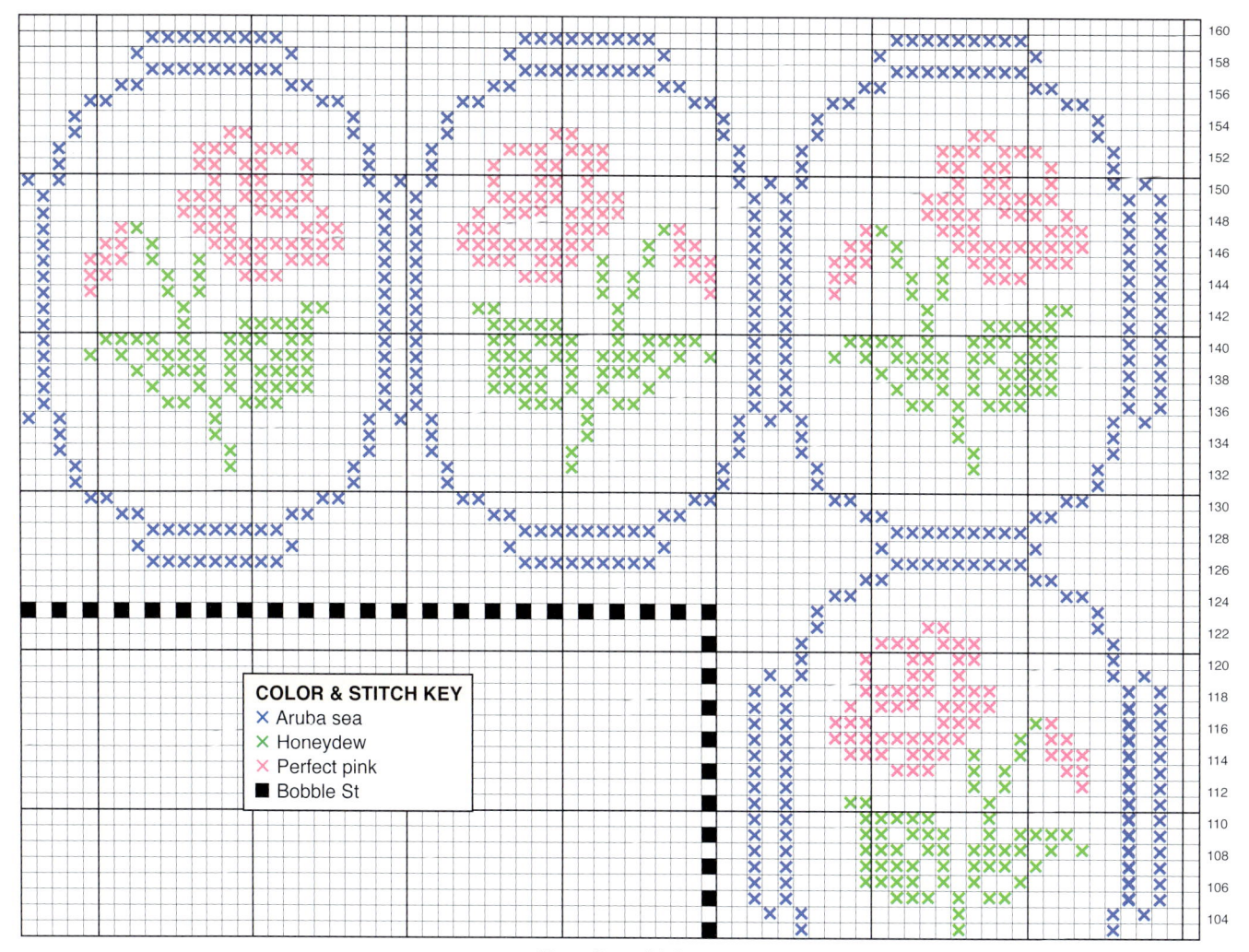

COLOR & STITCH KEY
× Aruba sea
× Honeydew
× Perfect pink
■ Bobble St

Hope Rose Afghan
Top Right Chart

in last st, ch 3 *(corner sp made)*, working across next side in ends of rows, pc in end of first row, [ch 1, sk next row, pc in next row] across to last st before next corner, ch 1, pc in last st, ch 3 *(corner sp made)*, working across next side in unused lps on opposite side of foundation ch, pc in first ch, [ch 1, sk next ch, pc in next ch] across to last ch before next corner, ch 1, pc in last ch, ch 3 *(corner sp made)*, working across next side in ends of rows, pc in end of first row, [ch 1, sk next row, pc in next row] across to last st before next corner, ch 1, pc in last st, ch 3 *(corner sp made)*, join in top of beg pc.

Rnd 2: Sl st in next ch-1 sp, **ch 3** *(see Pattern Notes)*, dc in same sp as beg ch-3, work 2 dc in ch-1 sp between rem pc and work (2 dc, ch 2, 2 dc) in each corner ch-3 sp around, join in beg dc.

Rnd 3: Sl st to 2nd dc of next 2-dc group, ch 1, sc in same dc as beg ch-1, working backward, sc in first dc of same 2-dc group *(beg crossed sc made)*, work **crossed sc** *(see Special Stitches)* in each 2-dc group and (dc, ch 2, dc) in each corner ch-2 sp around, join in beg sc.

Rnd 4: Ch 1, sc in each st around, working (dc, ch 2, dc) in each corner ch-2 sp around, join in beg sc.

Rnd 5: Sl st in next st, ch 1, sc in same st as beg ch-1, working backward, sc in joining sc, work crossed sc around, working (2 sc, ch 2, 2 sc) in each corner ch-2 sp, join in beg sc.

Rnd 6: Ch 3, dc in same sc as beg ch-3, sk next sc, [2 dc in next sc, sk next sc] around, working (2 dc, ch 2, 2 dc) in each corner ch-2 sp, join in 3rd ch of beg ch-3.

Rnd 7: Pc in first st, ch 1, work (pc, ch 1) in first dc of each 2-dc group around and work (pc, ch 1) twice in each corner ch-2 sp, join in top of beg ch-1.

Rnd 8: Sl st in next ch-1 sp, ch 3, dc in same sp as beg ch-3, **picot** *(see Special Stitches)*, work (2 dc, picot) in each rem ch-1 sp around, join in 3rd ch of beg ch-3. Fasten off. ■

COLOR & STITCH KEY
- × Aruba sea
- × Honeydew
- × Perfect pink
- ■ Bobble St

Hope Rose Afghan
Bottom Left Chart

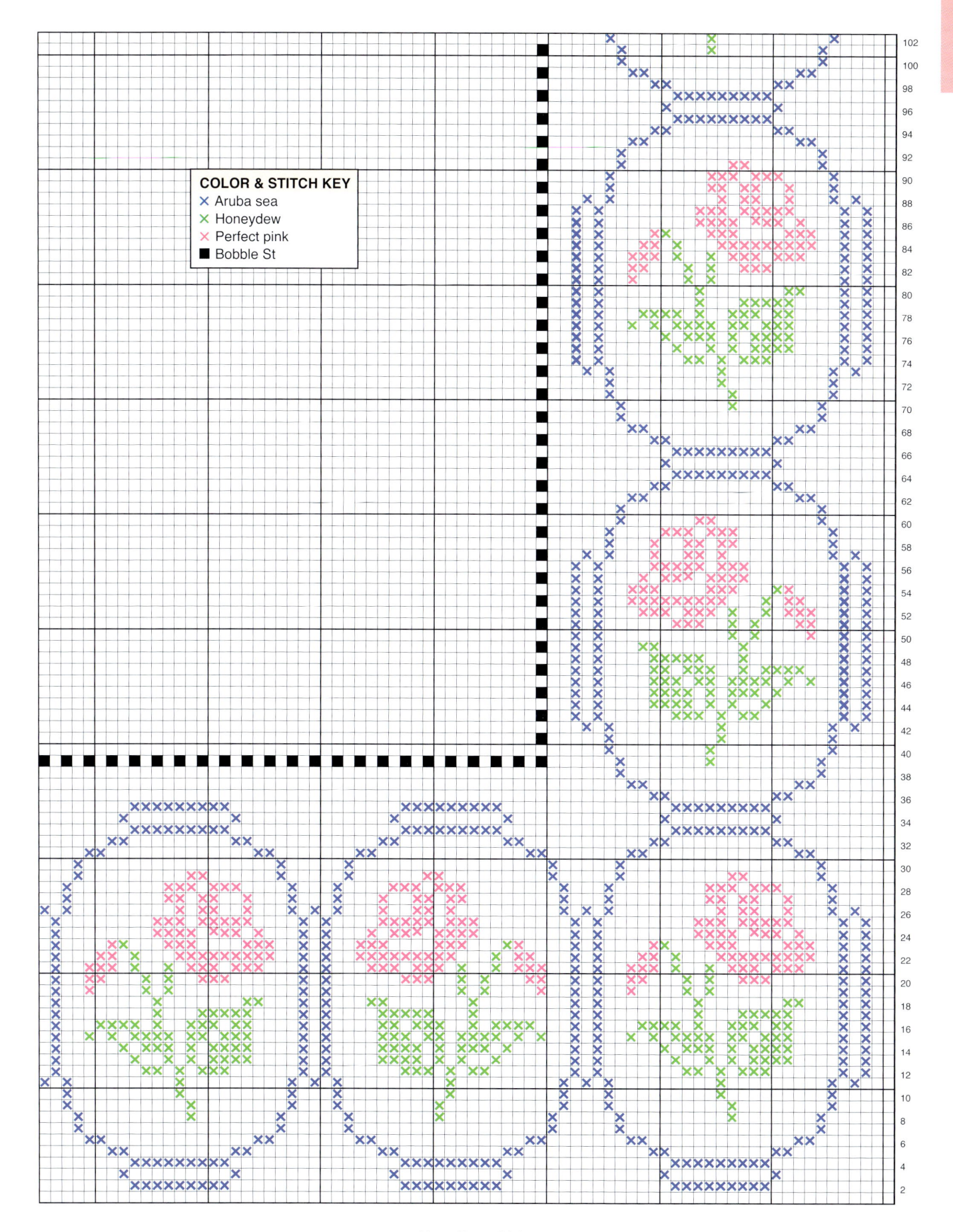

COLOR & STITCH KEY
- × Aruba sea
- × Honeydew
- × Perfect pink
- ■ Bobble St

Hope Rose Afghan
Bottom Right Chart

7

SUMMER BLUES Afghan

SKILL LEVEL

EASY

FINISHED MEASUREMENTS
49 inches wide x 60 inches long

MATERIALS
- Red Heart Super Saver medium (worsted) weight acrylic yarn (7 oz/364 yds/198g per skein):
    5 skeins #311 white
    2 skeins #385 royal
    1 skein each #235 lemon, #624 tea leaf, #381 light blue, #347 light periwinkle and #885 delft blue
- Size K/10½/6.5mm afghan crochet hook or size needed to obtain gauge
- Size J/10/6mm crochet hook
- Tapestry needle

GAUGE
With afghan hook: 15 sts and 13 rows = 4 inches

PATTERN NOTES
Weave in ends as work progresses.

Join with slip stitch as indicated unless otherwise stated.

AFGHAN
PANEL
Make 5.

Row 1: With afghan hook and white, ch 25, working from right to left, insert hook in 2nd ch from hook, yo, draw through ch, *insert hook in next ch, yo, draw through ch, rep from * across keeping all lps on hook (*25 lps on hook*), yo, draw through 1 lp on hook, **yo, draw through 2 lps on hook, rep from ** across until 1 lp rem on hook.

Rows 2–175: Working from right to left, insert hook in 2nd vertical st from hook, yo, draw through st, *insert hook in next vertical st, yo, draw through st, rep from * across keeping all lps on hook (*25 lps on hook*), yo, draw through 1 lp on hook, **yo, draw through 2 lps on hook, rep from ** across until 1 lp rem on hook.

Row 176: Sl st in each vertical st across. Fasten off.

EMBROIDERY
With RS facing and using **cross-stitches** *(see illustration)*, follow Chart A to cross-stitch design on 3 Panels. Follow Chart B to cross-stitch design on rem 2 Panels.

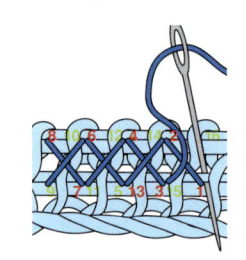

Cross-Stitch over Afghan Stitch

Note: *Make sure to count row-end st as a st when counting to start design.*

PANEL BORDER
Rnd 1: With RS facing and 1 short end at top, with size J hook, **join** *(see Pattern Notes)* light blue in top right-hand corner, ch 1, *sc in each of first 4 sts, **sc dec** *(see Stitch Guide)* in next 2 sts, [sc in each of next 4 sts, sc dec in next 2 sts] 3 times, ch 2 *(corner sp made)*, working across next side in ends of rows, sc in each of next 3 rows, [dc in next corresponding horizontal st 3 sts below, pulling dc up to current level of work, sc in each of next 6 rows] across to last 4 rows, dc in next corresponding horizontal st 3 sts below, pulling dc up to current level of work, sc in each of last 3 rows, ch 2 *(corner sp made)*, working across next side, rep from * once, join in beg sc. Fasten off.

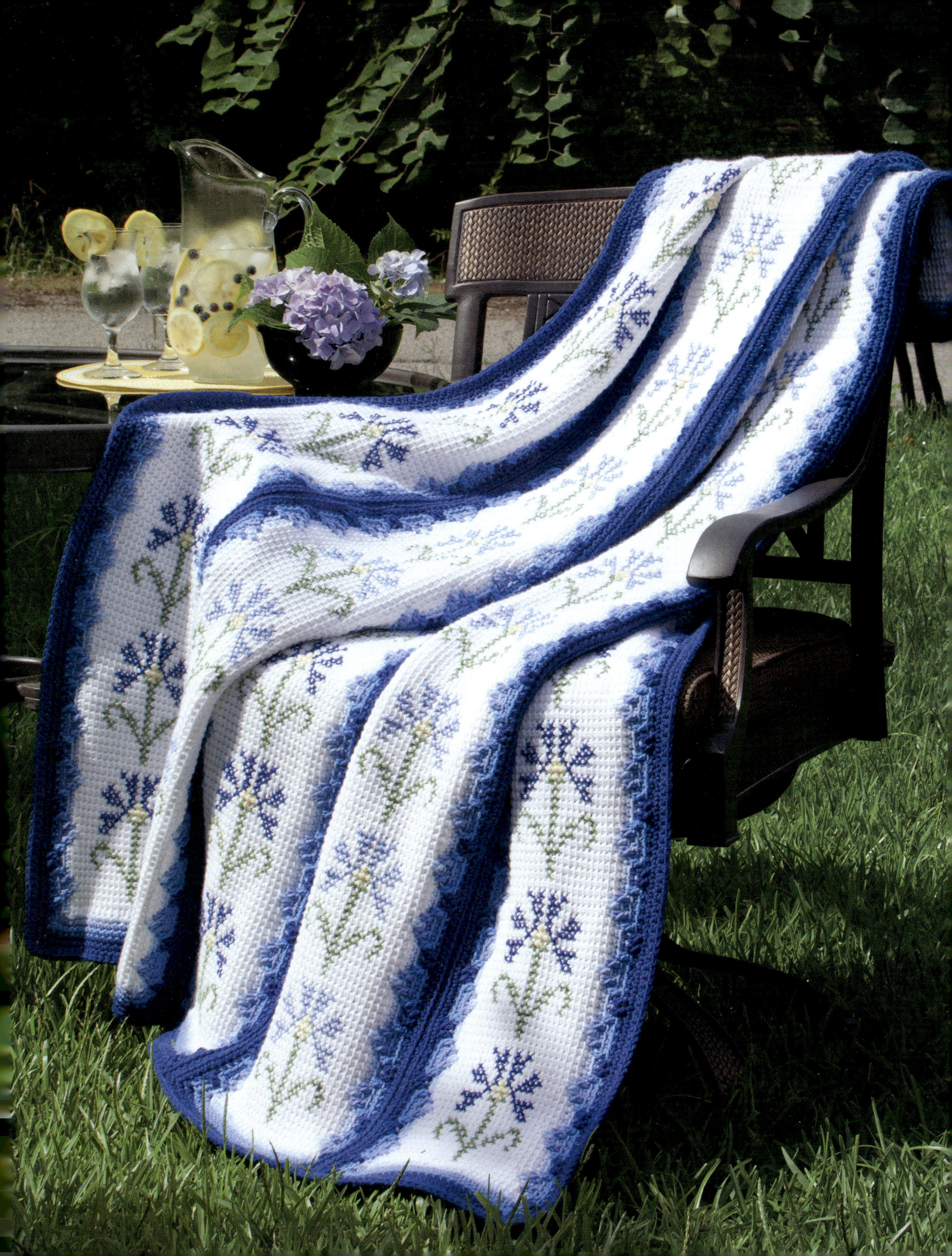

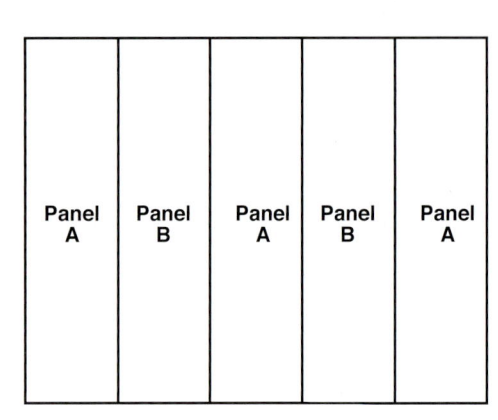

Summer Blues Afghan
Assembly Diagram

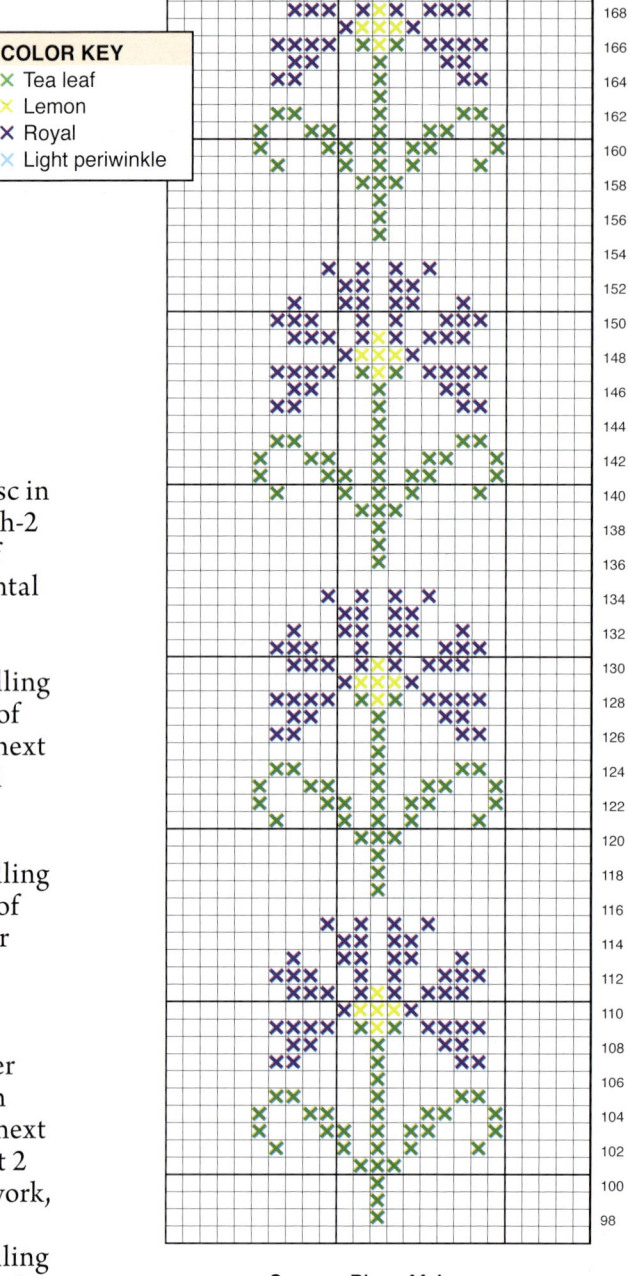

COLOR KEY
× Tea leaf
× Lemon
× Royal
× Light periwinkle

Summer Blues Afghan
Chart A Top of Panel

Rnd 2: Join light periwinkle in beg sc, ch 1, *sc in each sc across, (sc, ch 2, sc) in next corner ch-2 sp, sc in **back lp** (see Stitch Guide) of each of next 2 sc, [dc in next corresponding horizontal st 2 sts below, pulling dc up to current level of work, sc in back lp of next dc, dc in next corresponding horizontal st 2 sts below, pulling dc up to current level of work, sc in back lp of each of next 4 sc] across to last 5 sts before next corner, dc in next corresponding horizontal st 2 sts below, pulling dc up to current level of work, sc in back lp of next dc, dc in next corresponding horizontal st 2 sts below, pulling dc up to current level of work, sc in back lp of each of next 2 sc, (sc, ch 2, sc) in next corner ch-2 sp, rep from * around, join in beg sc. Fasten off.

Rnd 3: Join delft blue in top right-hand corner sc, ch 1, *sc in each sc across, (sc, ch 2, sc) in next corner ch-2 sp, sc in back lp of each of next 2 sc, [dc in next corresponding horizontal st 2 sts below, pulling dc up to current level of work, sc in back lp of each of next 3 sts, dc in next corresponding horizontal st 2 sts below, pulling dc up to current level of work, sc in back lp of each of next 2 sc] across to next corner, (sc, ch 2, sc) in next corner ch-2 sp, rep from * around, join in beg sc. Fasten off.

Rnd 4: Join royal in top right-hand corner sc, ch 1, *sc in each sc across, (sc, ch 2, sc) in corner ch-2 sp, sc in back lp of each of next 2 sc, dc in next corresponding horizontal st 2 sts below, pulling dc up to current level of work, [sc in back lp of each of next 5 sts, (dc in next corresponding horizontal st 2 sts below, pulling dc up to current level of work) twice] across to last 8 sts before next corner, sc in back lp of each of next 5 sts, dc in next corresponding horizontal st 2 sts below, pulling dc up to current level of work, sc in back lp of each of next 2 sts, (sc, ch 2, sc) in next corner ch-2 sp, rep from * around, join in beg sc.

Rnd 5: Ch 1, sc in each st around, working (sc, ch 2, sc) in each corner ch-2 sp, join in beg sc. Fasten off.

ASSEMBLY
Hold 2 Panels with RS tog and 1 long side at top. Beg and ending in corner sps, with size J hook and royal, sl st in **back lp** (see Stitch Guide) of sts across side.

Join rem Panels in same manner.

Summer Blues Afghan
Chart A Bottom of Panel

Summer Blues Afghan
Chart B Bottom of Panel

Summer Blues Afghan
Chart B Top of Panel

BORDER

Rnd 1: With RS facing and size J hook, join royal in top right-hand corner sc, ch 1, hdc in each sc and in ch-sp on each side of each joining seam around, working (hdc, ch 2, hdc) in each corner ch-2 sp, join in beg hdc. Fasten off. ■

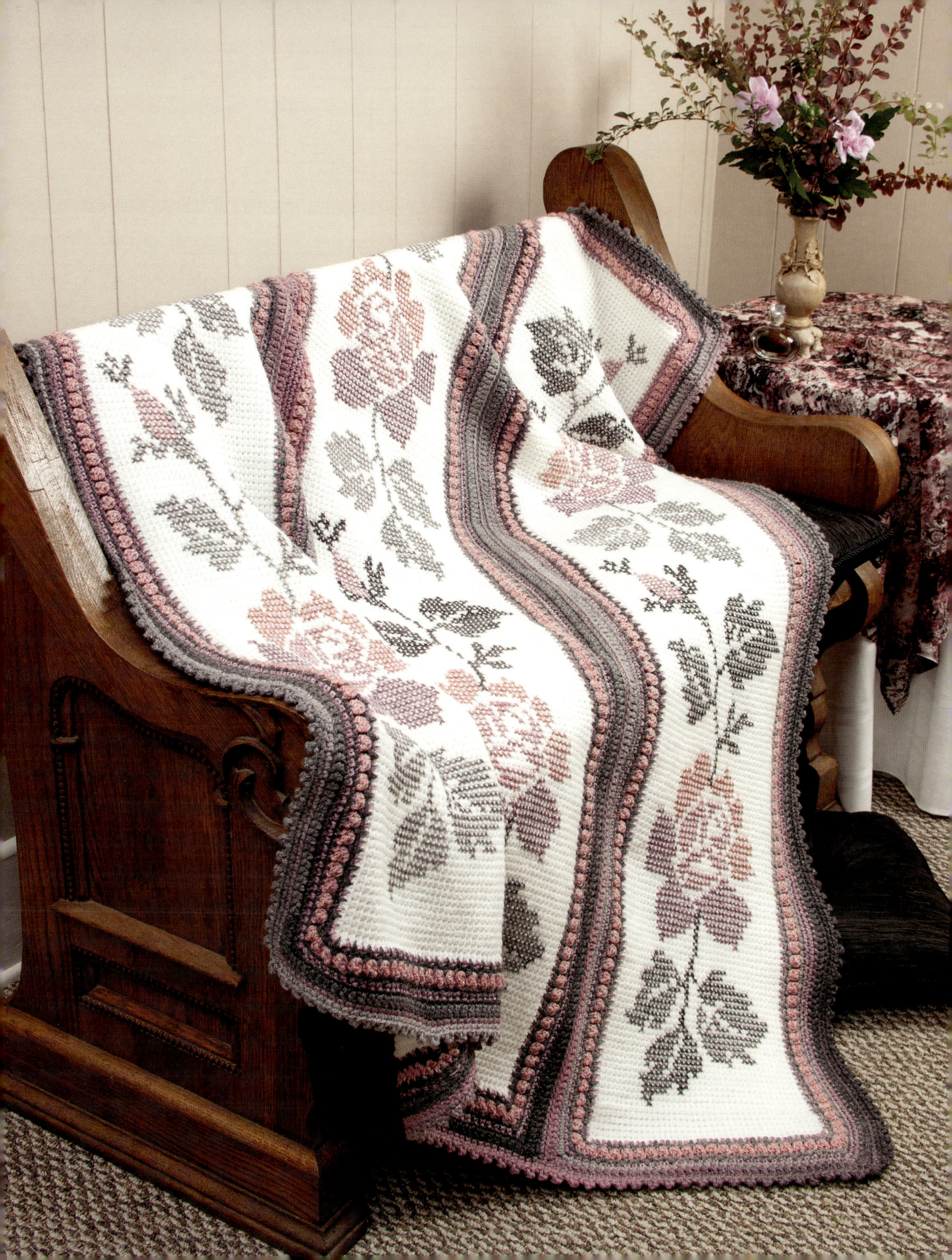

VICTORIAN ROSE *Afghan*

SKILL LEVEL
EASY

FINISHED MEASUREMENTS
49 inches wide x 60 inches long

MATERIALS
- Super fine (fingering) weight superwash wool/nylon/other fibers yarn:
  5¼ oz/573 yds/150g each purple and pink
  3½ oz/382 yds/100g coral
- Red Heart Super Saver medium (worsted) weight acrylic yarn (7 oz/364 yds/198g per skein):
  5 skeins #316 soft white
- Red Heart Boutique Midnight medium (worsted) weight acrylic/wool/nylon/metallic yarn (2½ oz/153 yds/70g per skein):
  7 skeins #1945 shadow
- Size J/10/6mm afghan crochet hook or size needed to obtain gauge
- Size J/10/6mm crochet hook
- Tapestry needle

GAUGE
With afghan hook: 15 sts and 13 rows = 4 inches

PATTERN NOTES
Weave in ends as work progresses.

Join with slip stitch as indicated unless otherwise stated.

Chain-3 at beginning of round counts as first double crochet unless otherwise stated.

SPECIAL STITCHES
Popcorn (pc): 3 dc in indicated st, drop lp from hook, insert hook from front to back under top 2 lps of first dc of group, pick up dropped lp and pull it through.

Picot: Ch 3, sl st in last st made.

AFGHAN
PANEL
Make 3.

Row 1: With afghan hook and soft white, ch 41, working from right to left, insert hook in 2nd ch from hook, yo, draw through ch, *insert hook in next ch, yo, draw through ch, rep from * across keeping all lps on hook *(41 lps on hook)*, yo, draw through 1 lp on hook, **yo, draw through 2 lps on hook, rep from ** across until 1 lp rem on hook.

Rows 2–196: Working from right to left, insert hook in 2nd vertical st from hook, yo, draw through st, *insert hook in next vertical st, yo, draw through st, rep from * across keeping all lps on hook *(41 lps on hook)*, yo, draw through 1 lp on hook, **yo, draw through 2 lps on hook, rep from ** across until 1 lp rem on hook.

Row 197: Sl st in each vertical st across. Fasten off.

EMBROIDERY
With RS facing and using **cross-stitches** *(see illustration)*, follow chart to cross-stitch design on each Panel.

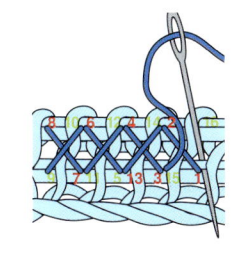

Cross-Stitch over Afghan Stitch

Note: *Make sure to count row-end st as a st when counting to start design.*

PANEL BORDER
Rnd 1: With RS facing and 1 short end at top, with size J hook, **join** *(see Pattern Notes)* 1 strand each of pink and purple held tog in top right-hand corner st, ch 1, sc in same st as beg

ch-1, [ch 1, sk next st, sc in next st] 19 times, sc in next st, ch 2 *(corner sp made)*, working across next side in ends of rows, sc in first row, [ch 1, sk next row, sc in next row] across to last row, sc in last row, ch 2 *(corner sp made)*, working across next side in unused lps on opposite side of foundation ch, sc in next ch, [ch 1, sk next ch, sc in next ch] 19 times, sc in last ch, ch 2 *(corner sp made)*, working across next side in ends of rows, sc in first row, [ch 1, sk next row, sc in next row] across to last row, sc in last row, ch 2 *(corner sp made)*, join in beg sc. Fasten off.

Rnd 2: Join shadow in beg sc, ch 1, sc in same st as beg ch-1, *[hdc in next corresponding st 2 rnds below on Panel edge, pulling hdc up to current level of work, sc in next sc] across to last sc before next corner, sc in last sc, (sc, ch 2, sc) in corner ch-2 sp, sc in next sc, [hdc in next corresponding st 2 rnds below on Panel edge, pulling hdc up to current level of work, sc in next sc] across to last sc before next corner, sc in last sc, (sc, ch 2, sc) in corner ch-2 sp**, sc in next sc, rep from * once ending rep at **, join in beg sc. Fasten off.

Rnd 3: With 1 strand each of pink and coral held tog, join in corner ch-2 sp, (**pc**—*see Special Stitches*, ch 2, pc) in same corner ch-2 sp, *[ch 2, sk next st, pc in next sc] across to last 2 sc before next corner, ch 2, sk last 2 sc, (pc, ch 2, pc) in corner ch-2 sp, [ch 2, sk next st, pc in next sc] across to last 2 sc before corner, sk last 2 sc**, (pc, ch 2, pc) in corner ch-2 sp, rep from * once, ending rep at **, join in beg pc. Fasten off.

Rnd 4: Join shadow in beg pc, ch 1, sc in each pc and each ch-2 sp around, working (sc, ch 2, sc) in each corner ch-2 sp, join in beg sc. Fasten off.

Rnd 5: Join 1 strand each of pink and purple held tog in top right-hand corner ch-2 sp, ch 1, *(sc, ch 2, sc) in corner ch-2 sp, [sk next sc, sc in each of next 3 sc] 11 times, sk next sc, (sc, ch 2, sc) in next corner ch-2 sp, sc in each sc across to next corner ch-2 sp, rep from * once, join in beg sc. Fasten off.

Rnd 6: Join shadow in first sc in top right-hand corner, ch 1, sc in each sc around, working (sc, ch 2, sc) in each corner ch-2 sp, join in beg sc.

Rnd 7: Ch 3 *(see Pattern Notes)*, dc in each sc around, working (2 dc, ch 2, 2 dc) in corner ch-2 sp, join in 3rd ch of beg ch-3. Fasten off.

ASSEMBLY
Hold 2 Panels with RS tog and 1 long side at top, with size J hook and working through both thicknesses, join shadow in first ch of right-hand corner ch-2 sp, ch 1, sc in same ch as beg ch-1 and in next ch, working across side, dc in each sc and sc in each ch of each rem corner ch-2 sp across. Fasten off.

Join rem Panels in same manner.

BORDER
Rnd 1: With RS facing and size J hook, join shadow in top right-hand corner ch-2 sp, ch 1, 2 sc in same corner sp as beg ch-1, working around outer edge, sc in each dc and in ch sp on each side of joining seams and 2 sc in each rem corner ch-2 sp, join in beg sc.

Rnd 2: Ch 1, sc in same sc as beg ch-1 and in next sc, **picot** *(see Special Stitches)*, *sc in each of next 2 sc, picot, rep from * around, join in beg sc. Fasten off. ■

COLOR KEY
× 2 strands of coral, 1 strand of pink held together
× 3 strands of pink held together
× 2 strands of purple, 1 strand of pink held together
× Shadow

Victorian Rose Afghan
Bottom of Panel Chart

Victorian Rose Afghan
Top of Panel Chart

PENNSYLVANIA DUTCH *Afghan*

SKILL LEVEL

EASY

FINISHED MEASUREMENTS
51 inches wide x 68 inches long

MATERIALS
- Red Heart Super Saver medium (worsted) weight acrylic yarn (7 oz/364 yds/198g per skein):
  5 skeins #311 white
  2 skeins each #624 tea leaf, #631 light sage and #633 dark sage
  1 skein #319 cherry red
- Size K/10½/6.5mm afghan crochet hook or size needed to obtain gauge
- Size I/9/5.5mm crochet hook
- Tapestry needle

4 MEDIUM

GAUGE
With afghan hook: 14 sts and 12 rows = 4 inches

PATTERN NOTES
Weave in ends as work progresses.

Join with slip stitch as indicated unless otherwise stated.

Chain-3 at beginning of round counts as first double crochet unless otherwise stated.

AFGHAN
BLOCK
Make 20.

Row 1: With afghan hook and white, ch 33, working from right to left, insert hook in 2nd ch from hook, yo, draw through ch, *insert hook in next ch, yo, draw through ch, rep from * across keeping all lps on hook (*33 lps on hook*), yo, draw through 1 lp on hook, **yo, draw through 2 lps on hook, rep from ** across until 1 lp rem on hook.

Rows 2–31: Working from right to left, insert hook in 2nd vertical st from hook, yo, draw through st, *insert hook in next vertical st, yo, draw through st, rep from * across keeping all lps on hook (*33 lps on hook*), yo, draw through

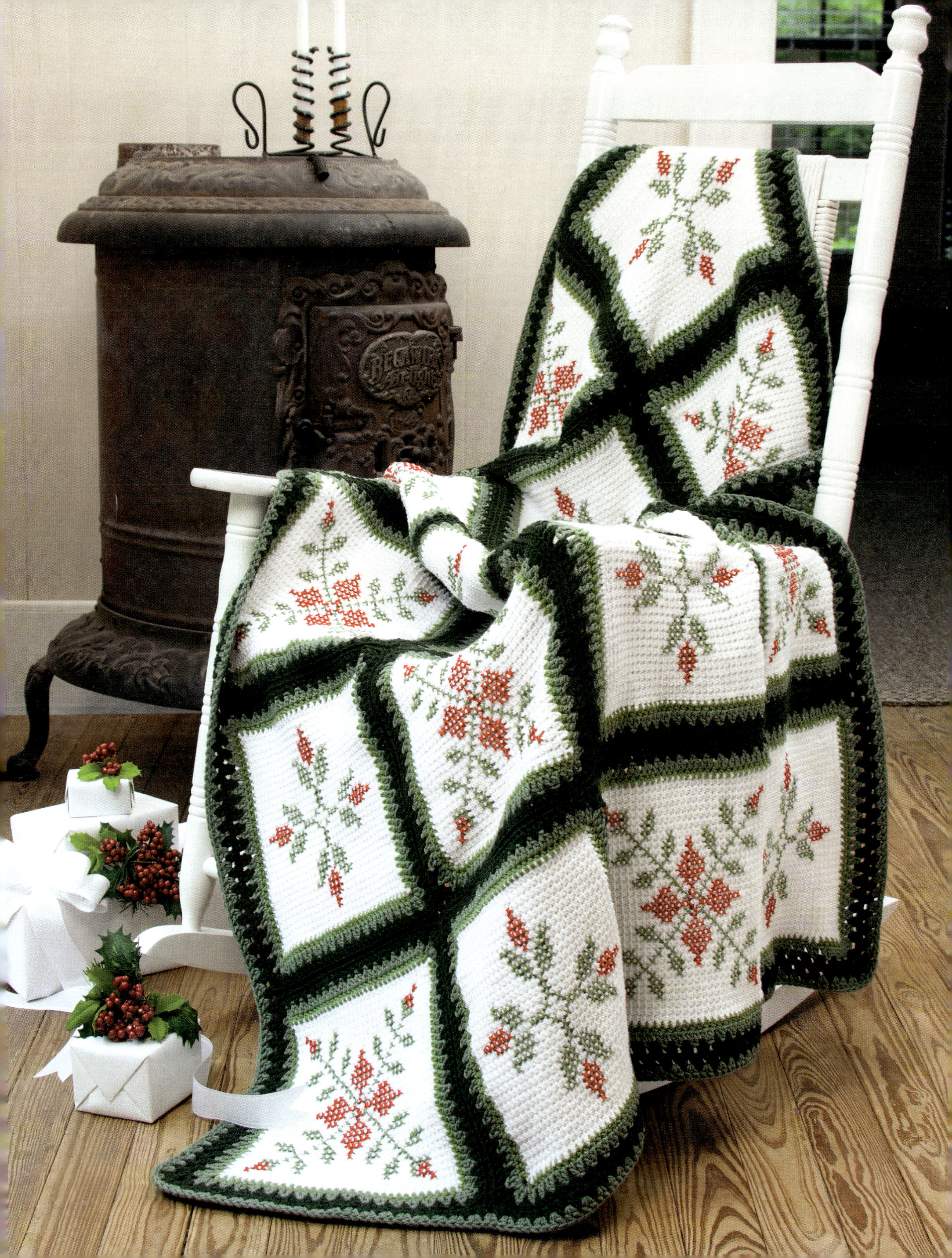

1 lp on hook, **yo, draw through 2 lps on hook, rep from ** across until 1 lp rem on hook.

Row 32: Sl st in each vertical st across. Fasten off.

EMBROIDERY
With RS facing and using **cross-stitches** (see illustration), follow Chart A to cross-stitch design on 10 blocks. Follow Chart B to cross-stitch design on rem 10 blocks.

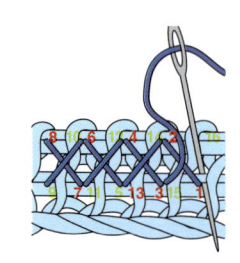

Cross-Stitch over Afghan Stitch

Note: Make sure to count row-end st as a st when counting to start design.

BLOCK BORDER
Rnd 1: With RS facing and size I hook, **join** (see Pattern Notes) tea leaf in top right-hand corner st, ch 1, hdc in each st across, ch 2 (corner sp made), working across next side in ends of rows, hdc in each row across, ch 2 (corner sp made), working across next side in unused lps on opposite side of foundation ch, hdc in each ch across, ch 2 (corner sp made), working across next side in ends of rows, hdc in each row, ch 2 (corner sp made), join in beg hdc. Fasten off.

Rnd 2: Join light sage in beg hdc, **ch 3** (see Pattern Notes), dc in each hdc around, working (2 dc, ch 2, 2 dc) in each corner ch-2 sp, join in 3rd ch of beg ch-3. Fasten off.

Rnd 3: Join dark sage in top right-hand corner ch-2 sp, ch 3, (dc, ch 2, 2 dc) in same ch sp, *[sk next 2 dc, 2 dc between sk 2 dc and next dc] 17 times, sk next 2 dc, (2 dc, ch 2, 2 dc) in next corner ch-2 sp, [sk next 2 dc, 2 dc between sk 2 dc and next dc] 16 times, sk next 3 dc**, (2 dc, ch 2, 2 dc) in next corner ch-2 sp, rep from * around, ending last rep at **, join in 3rd ch of beg ch-3. Fasten off.

ASSEMBLY
Following Assembly Diagram, hold 2 Blocks with RS tog. Beg and ending in corner sps and working through both thicknesses, with size I hook and dark sage, sc in **back lp** (see Stitch Guide) of sts across 1 side. Join rem Blocks in same manner, with 5 rows of 4 Blocks each.

BORDER
Rnd 1: With RS facing and size I hook, join dark sage in top right-hand corner ch-2 sp, ch 3, 5 dc in same corner ch-2 sp, work 2 dc between each 2-dc group and in ch sp on each side of each joining seam around and work 6 dc in each rem corner ch-2 sp, join in 3rd ch of beg ch-3. Fasten off.

Rnd 2: Join light sage between any group of 2 dc, ch 3, dc in same sp, work 2 dc between each 2-dc group around, join in 3rd ch of beg ch-3. Fasten off. ■

A	B	A	B
B	A	B	A
A	B	A	B
B	A	B	A
A	B	A	B

Pennsylvania Dutch Afghan
Assembly Diagram

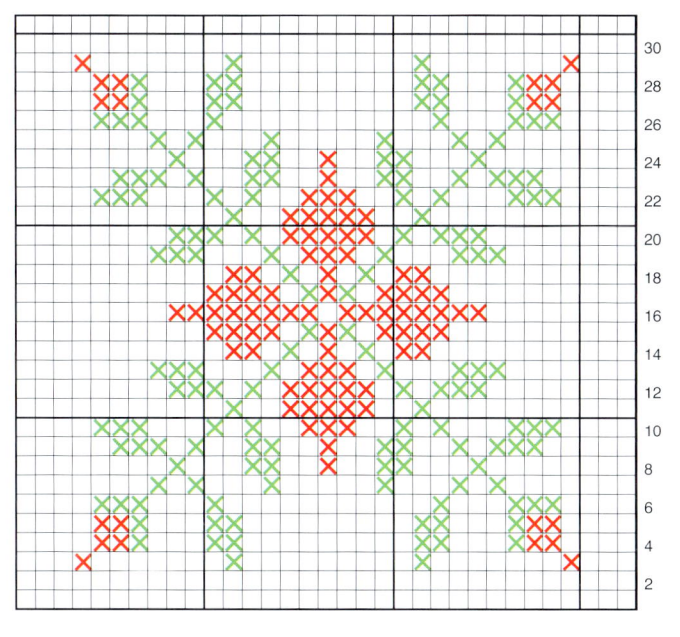

COLOR KEY
× Tea leaf
× Cherry red

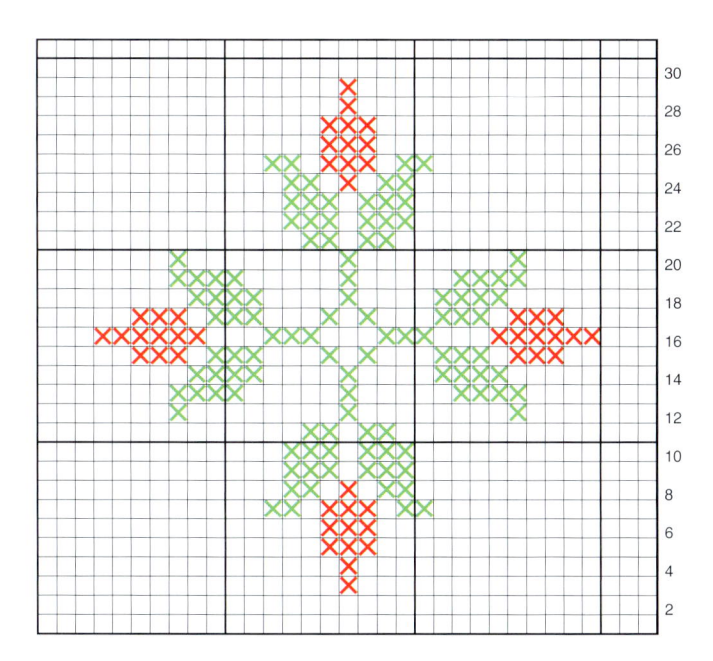

Pennsylvania Dutch Afghan
Chart A

Pennsylvania Dutch Afghan
Chart B

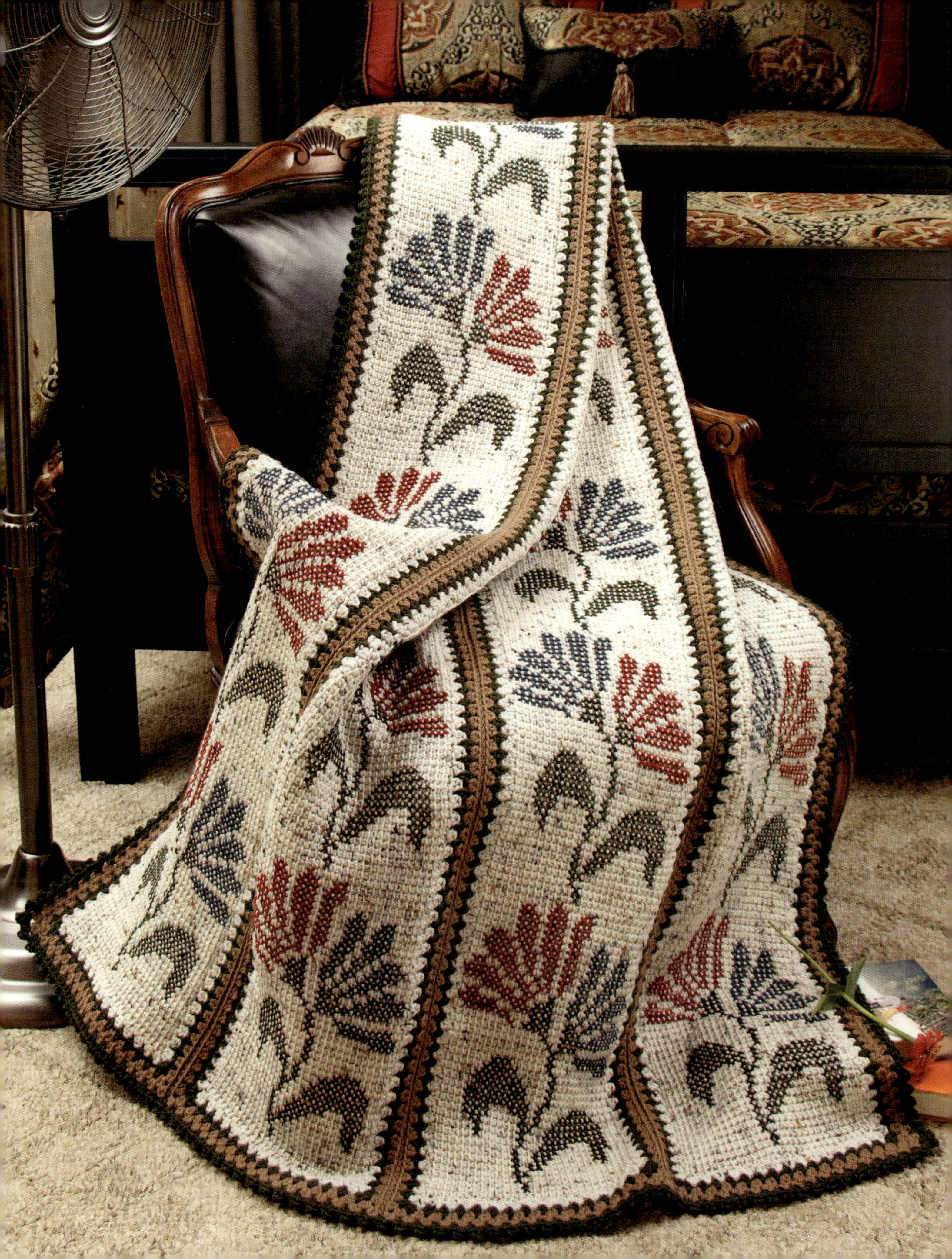

FARMHOUSE Afghan

SKILL LEVEL
EASY

FINISHED MEASUREMENTS
45 inches wide x 69 inches long

MATERIALS
- Red Heart Super Saver medium (worsted) weight acrylic yarn (solids: 7 oz/364 yds/198g per skein; flecks: 5 oz/260 yds/141g per skein):
    8 skeins #4313 Aran fleck
    2 skeins #633 dark sage
    1 skein each #360 café latte,
    #376 burgundy and #380 Windsor blue
- Size K/10½/6.5mm afghan crochet hook or size needed to obtain gauge
- Size I/9/5.5mm crochet hook
- Tapestry needle

GAUGE
With afghan hook: 14 sts and 13 rows = 4 inches

PATTERN NOTES
Weave in ends as work progresses.

Join with slip stitch as indicated unless otherwise stated.

SPECIAL STITCH
Picot: Ch 3, sl st in last st made.

AFGHAN
PANEL
Make 4.

Row 1: With afghan hook and Aran fleck, ch 31, working from right to left, insert hook in 2nd ch from hook, yo, draw through ch, *insert hook in next ch, yo, draw through ch, rep from * across keeping all lps on hook *(31 lps on hook)*, yo, draw through 1 lp on hook, **yo, draw through 2 lps on hook, rep from ** across until 1 lp rem on hook.

Rows 2–204: Working from right to left, insert hook in 2nd vertical st from hook, yo, draw through st, *insert hook in next vertical st, yo, draw through st, rep from * across keeping all lps on hook *(31 lps on hook)*, yo, draw through 1 lp on hook, **yo, draw through 2 lps on hook, rep from ** across until 1 lp rem on hook.

Row 205: Sl st in each vertical st across. Fasten off.

EMBROIDERY
With RS facing and using **cross-stitches** *(see illustration)*, follow chart to cross-stitch design on each Panel.

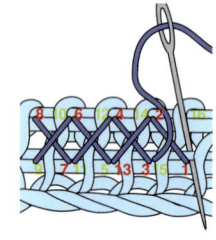

Cross-Stitch over Afghan Stitch

Note: *Make sure to count row-end st as a st when counting to start design.*

PANEL BORDER
Rnd 1: With RS facing and size I hook, **join** *(see Pattern Notes)* Aran fleck in top right-hand corner st, ch 1, 2 hdc in first st, *[sk next st, 2 hdc in next st]13 times, sk next 2 sts, 2 hdc in last st, ch 2 *(corner sp made)*, working across next side in ends of rows, 2 hdc in end of first row, [sk next row, 2 hdc in end of next row] across to last row, 2 hdc in last row, ch 2 *(corner sp made)***, 2 hdc in next st, rep from * once, ending rep at **, join in beg hdc. Fasten off.

Rnd 2: Join dark sage in top right-hand corner ch-2 sp, ch 1, (2 hdc, ch 2, 2 hdc) in same sp, work 2 hdc between each group of 2 hdc around and work (2 hdc, ch 2, 2 hdc) in each rem corner ch-2 sp, join in beg hdc. Fasten off.

Rnd 3: With café latte, rep rnd 2.

ASSEMBLY
Hold 2 Panels with RS tog and 1 long side at top. Beg and ending in corner sps and working through both thicknesses, with size I hook and café latte, sl st in **back lp** *(see Stitch Guide)* of sts across side.

Join rem Panels in same manner.

BORDER
Rnd 1: With RS facing and size I hook, join café latte in top right-hand corner ch-2 sp, ch 1, (2 hdc, ch 2, 2 hdc) in corner ch-2 sp, work 2 hdc between each group of 2 hdc and in ch sp on each side of each joining seam around and work (2 hdc, ch 2, 2 hdc) in each rem corner ch-2 sp, join in beg hdc. Fasten off.

Rnd 2: Join dark sage in top right-hand corner ch-2 sp, ch 1, (2 hdc, **picot**—*see Special Stitch*) twice in same sp, (2 hdc, picot) between each group of 2 hdc around and work (2 hdc, picot) twice in each rem corner ch-2 sp, join in beg hdc. Fasten off. ■

COLOR KEY
× Dark sage
× Burgundy
× Windsor blue

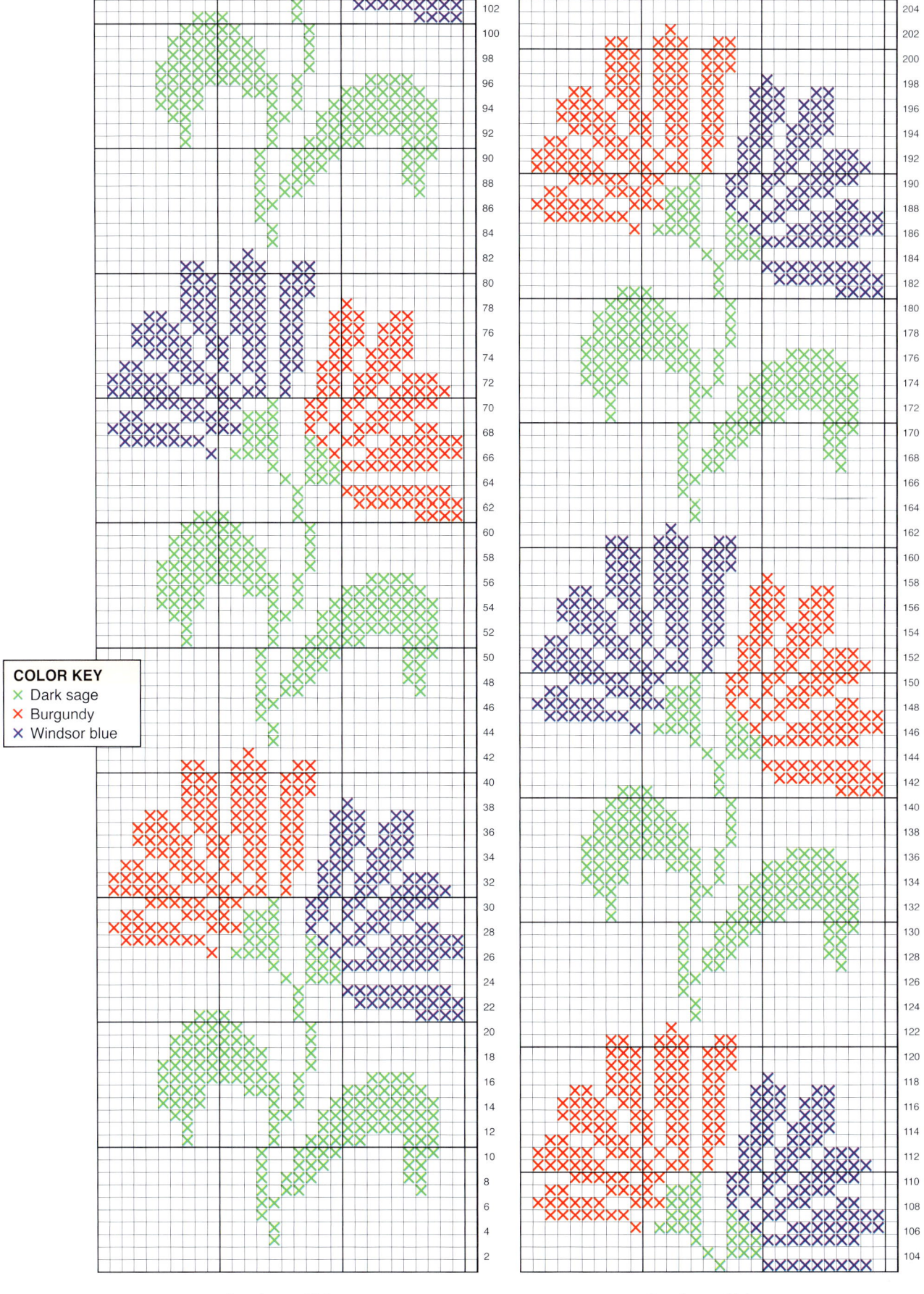

Farmhouse Afghan
Bottom of Panel Chart

Farmhouse Afghan
Top of Panel Chart

23

SPRING BUTTERFLY Afghan

SKILL LEVEL
EASY

FINISHED MEASUREMENTS
46 inches wide x 64 inches long

MATERIALS
- Red Heart Super Saver medium (worsted) weight acrylic yarn (7 oz/364 yds/198g per skein):
  7 skeins #311 white
  1 skein each #235 lemon, #505 Aruba sea, #624 tea leaf, #885 delft blue and #312 black
- Size J/10/6mm afghan crochet hook or size needed to obtain gauge
- Size I/9/5.5mm crochet hook
- Tapestry needle

4 MEDIUM

GAUGE
With afghan hook: 16 sts and 13 rows = 4 inches

PATTERN NOTES
Weave in ends as work progresses.

Join with slip stitch as indicated unless otherwise stated.

Chain-3 at beginning of round counts as first double crochet unless otherwise stated.

SPECIAL STITCHES
Crossed single crochet (crossed sc): Sk next st, sc in next st, working backward, sc in previously sk st.

Picot: Ch 3, sl st in last st made.

AFGHAN
PANEL
Make 3.

Row 1: With afghan hook and white, ch 31, working from right to left, insert hook in 2nd ch from hook, yo, draw through ch, *insert hook in next ch, yo, draw through ch, rep from * across keeping all lps on hook *(31 lps on hook)*, yo, draw through 1 lp on hook, **yo, draw through 2 lps on hook, rep from ** across until 1 lp rem on hook.

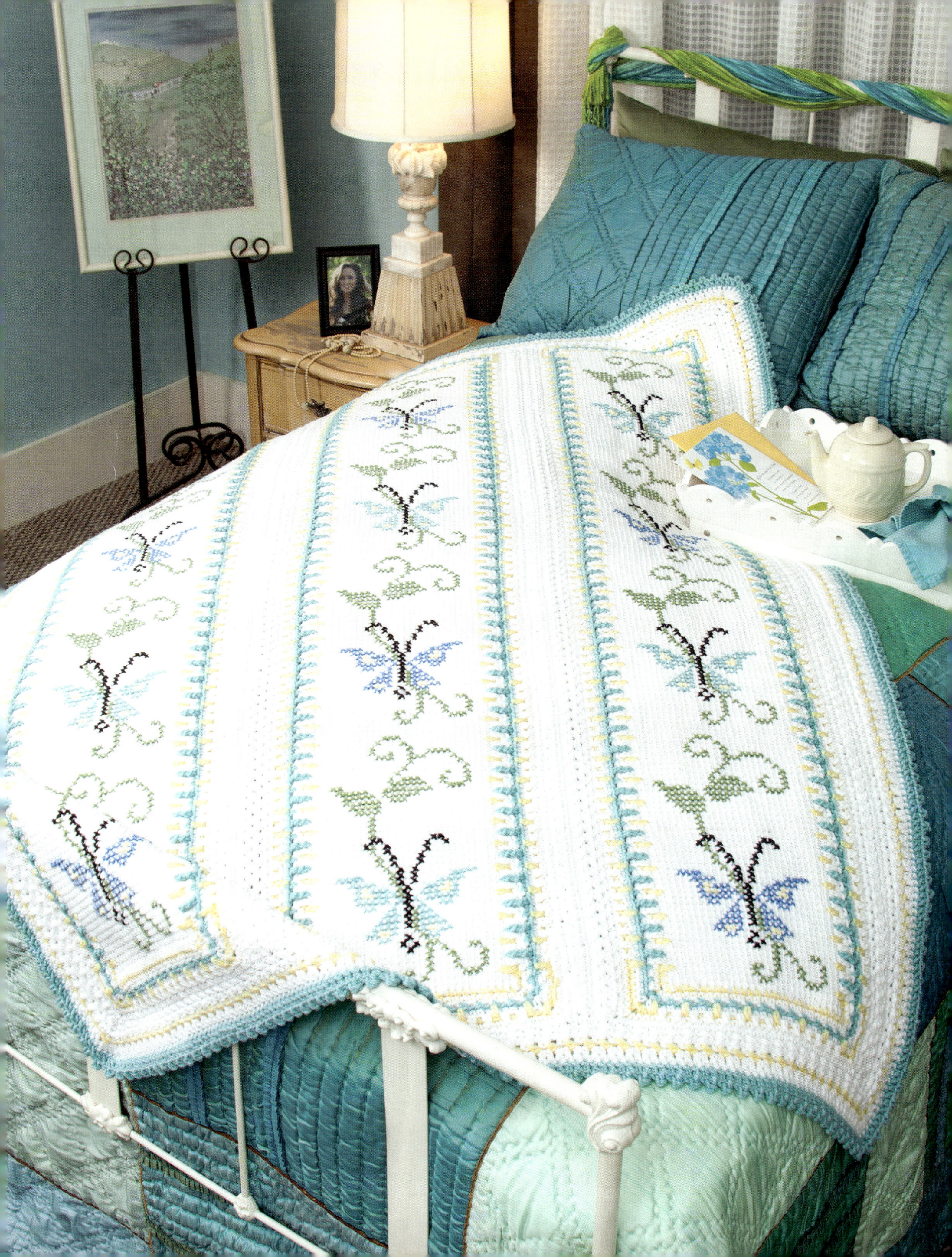

Rows 2–181: Working from right to left, insert hook in 2nd vertical st from hook, yo, draw through st, *insert hook in next vertical st, yo, draw through st, rep from * across keeping all lps on hook (*31 lps on hook*), yo, draw through 1 lp on hook, **yo, draw through 2 lps on hook, rep from ** across until 1 lp rem on hook.

Row 182: Sl st in each vertical st across. Fasten off.

EMBROIDERY
With RS facing and using **cross-stitches** (*see illustration*), follow Chart A to cross-stitch design on 2 Panels. Follow Chart B to cross-stitch design on rem Panel.

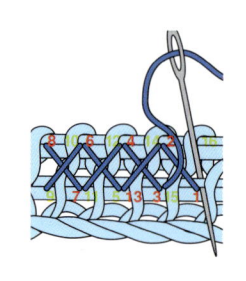

Cross-Stitch over Afghan Stitch

Note: Make sure to count row-end st as a st when counting to start design.

PANEL BORDER
Rnd 1: Hold 1 Panel with RS facing and long side at top, with size I hook, **join** (*see Pattern Notes*) lemon in end of first row in right-hand corner, ch 1, sc in same row as beg ch-1 and in next row, *dc in next corresponding horizontal st 3 sts below, pulling dc up to current level of work, [sc in each of next 3 rows, dc in next corresponding horizontal st 3 sts below, pulling dc up to current level of work] across to last 2 rows before next corner, sc in each of last 2 rows, ch 2 (*corner sp made*), *working across next side in unused lps on opposite side of foundation ch, (sc in each of next 4 chs, sk next ch) 5 times, sc in each of next 5 chs, ch 2 (*corner sp made*)*, working across next side in ends of rows, sc in each of first 2 rows, rep from * to * once, join in beg sc. Fasten off.

Rnd 2: Join white in beg sc, ch 1, *sc in each of next 2 sc, sc in next dc, [dc in next corresponding horizontal st 2 sts below, pulling dc up to current level of work, sc in next sc, dc in next corresponding horizontal st 2 sts below, pulling dc up to current level of work, sc in next dc] across to last 2 sts before next corner ch-2 sp, sc in each of last 2 sc, (sc, ch 2, sc) in corner ch-2 sp, sc in each sc across to next corner ch-2 sp, (sc, ch 2, sc) in corner ch-2 sp, rep from * once, join in beg sc. Fasten off.

Rnd 3: Join Aruba sea in beg sc, ch 1, sc in beg sc, *ch 1, sk next sc, [sc in next sc, ch 1, sk next dc, tr in next corresponding horizontal st 3 sts below, pulling tr up to current level of work, ch 1, sk next dc] across to last 4 sc before next corner ch-2 sp, (sc in next sc, ch 1, sk next sc) twice, (sc, ch 2, sc) in corner ch-2 sp, [ch 1, sk next sc, sc in next sc] 13 times, ch 1, sk next sc, (sc, ch 2, sc) in next corner ch-2 sp, ch 1, sk next sc**, sc in next sc, rep from * once, ending rep at **, join in beg sc. Fasten off.

Rnd 4: Join white in **back lp** (*see Stitch Guide*) of beg sc, ch 1, working in back lp of sts, sc in each st and in each ch-1 sp around, working (sc, ch 2, sc) in each corner ch-2 sp, join in beg sc.

Rnd 5: Join lemon in back lp of beg sc, ch 1, sc in back lp of same sc as beg ch-1 and in back lp of next sc, dc in **front lp** (*see Stitch Guide*) of next corresponding horizontal st 2 sts below, pulling dc up to current level of work, *[sc in back lp of each of next 3 sc, dc in front lp of next corresponding horizontal st 2 sts below, pulling dc up to current level of work] across to last 5 sc before next corner, sc in back lp of each of next 5 sc, (sc, ch 2, sc) in next corner ch-2 sp, sc in back lp of next sc, dc in front lp of next corresponding horizontal st 2 sts below, pulling dc up to current level of work, [sc in back lp of each of next 3 sc, dc in front lp of next corresponding horizontal st 2 sts below, pulling dc up to current level of work] across to last sc before next corner, sc in back lp of next sc, (sc, ch 2, sc) in next corner ch-2 sp*, sc in back lp of each of next 5 sc, dc in front lp of next corresponding horizontal st 2 sts below, pulling dc up to current level of work, rep from * to * to last 3 sc, sc in back lp of each of last 3 sc, join in back lp of beg sc. Fasten off.

Rnd 6: Join white in beg sc, ch 1, sc in each of first 2 sc, *[sc in next dc, dc in next corresponding horizontal st 2 rnds below, pulling dc up to current level of work, sc in next sc, dc in next corresponding horizontal st 2 rnds below, pulling dc up to current level of work] across to last 7 sts before next corner, sc in each of last 7 sts, (sc, ch 2, sc) in next corner ch-2 sp, sc in each of next 2 sc, [sc in next dc, dc in next corresponding horizontal st 2 rnds below, pulling dc up to current level of work, sc in next sc, dc in next corresponding horizontal st 2 rnds below, pulling dc up to current level of work] across to last 3 sts before next corner, sc in each of last 3 sts, (sc, ch 2, sc) in next corner ch-2 sp*, sc in each of next 6 sc, rep from * to * to last 4 sts, sc in each of last 4 sts. Fasten off.

SIDE BORDER

Row 1: Hold Panel with RS facing and 1 long side at top, with size I hook, join white in right-hand corner ch-2 sp, ch 1, sc in same sp as beg ch-1, *work **crossed sc** (see Special Stitches) across to last sc before next corner ch-2 sp, sc in last sc, sc in next corner ch-2 sp, turn.

Row 2: Ch 1, sc in each of first 2 sc, work crossed sc across to last sc, sc in last sc, turn.

Row 3: Ch 1, sc in first sc, work crossed sc across. Fasten off.

Work Side Border on opposite long side.

ASSEMBLY

Hold 2 Panels with RS tog and 1 long side at top. Beg and ending in corner sps, working through both thicknesses and with white, sl st in **back lp** (see Stitch Guide) of sts across side.

Join rem Panels in same manner.

BORDER

Rnd 1: With RS facing and 1 short end at top, with size I hook, join white in first sc in right-hand corner, ch 1, sc in same sc as beg ch-1, sc in each sc and in each row-end st across to next corner, ch 2 (corner sp made), working across next side, sc in each sc across to next corner, ch 2 (corner sp made), working in unused lps on opposite side of foundation ch, sc in each ch across to next corner, ch 2 (corner sp made), working across next side, sc in each sc across to next corner, ch 2 (corner sp made), join in beg sc.

Rnd 2: Ch 1, *work crossed sc across to last sc from next corner, sc in last sc, (sc, ch 2, sc) in corner ch-2 sp, work crossed sc across to next corner ch-2 sp, (sc, ch 2, sc) in corner ch-2 sp, rep from * around, join in beg sc, **turn**.

Rnd 3: Working on WS, ch 1, sc in first sc, (sc, ch 2, sc) in corner ch-2 sp, sc in next sc, work crossed sc across to last sc before next corner, sc in last sc, (sc, ch 2, sc) in corner ch-2 sp, work crossed sc across to last sc before next corner, sc in last sc, (sc, ch 2, sc) in corner ch-2 sp, sc in next sc, work crossed sc across to last sc before next corner, sc in last sc, (sc, ch 2, sc) in corner ch-2 sp, work crossed sc across to beg sc, join in beg sc. Fasten off. **Turn.**

Rnd 4: With RS facing, join lemon in top right-hand corner ch-2 sp, ch 1, (sc, ch 2, sc) in corner ch-2 sp, sc in next sc, *work crossed sc across to last sc before next corner, sc in last sc, (sc, ch 2, sc) in corner ch-2 sp, work crossed sc across to next corner**, (sc, ch 2, sc) in next corner ch-2 sp, rep from * once, ending rep at **, join in beg sc. Fasten off.

Rnd 5: Join white in top right-hand corner ch-2 sp, **ch 3** (see Pattern Notes), 5 dc in same corner sp as beg ch-3, sk next 2 sc, [2 dc in next sc, sk next sc] across to next corner ch-2 sp, 6 dc in corner ch-2 sp, [2 dc in next sc, sk next sc] across to last 2 sc before next corner, sk last 2 sc, 6 dc in next corner ch-2 sp, sk next sc, [2 dc in next sc, sk next sc] across to next corner ch-2 sp, 6 dc in corner ch-2 sp, sk next sc, [2 dc in next sc, sk next sc] across to last 2 sc, sk last 2 sc, join in 3rd ch of beg ch-3. Fasten off.

Rnd 6: Join Aruba sea in 3rd ch of beg ch-3, ch 3, dc in next dc, **picot** (see Special Stitches), *dc in each of next 2 dc, picot, rep from * around, join in 3rd ch of beg ch-3. Fasten off. ∎

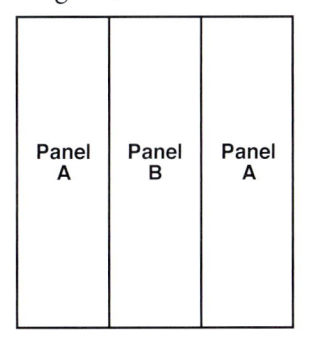

Spring Butterfly Afghan
Assembly Diagram

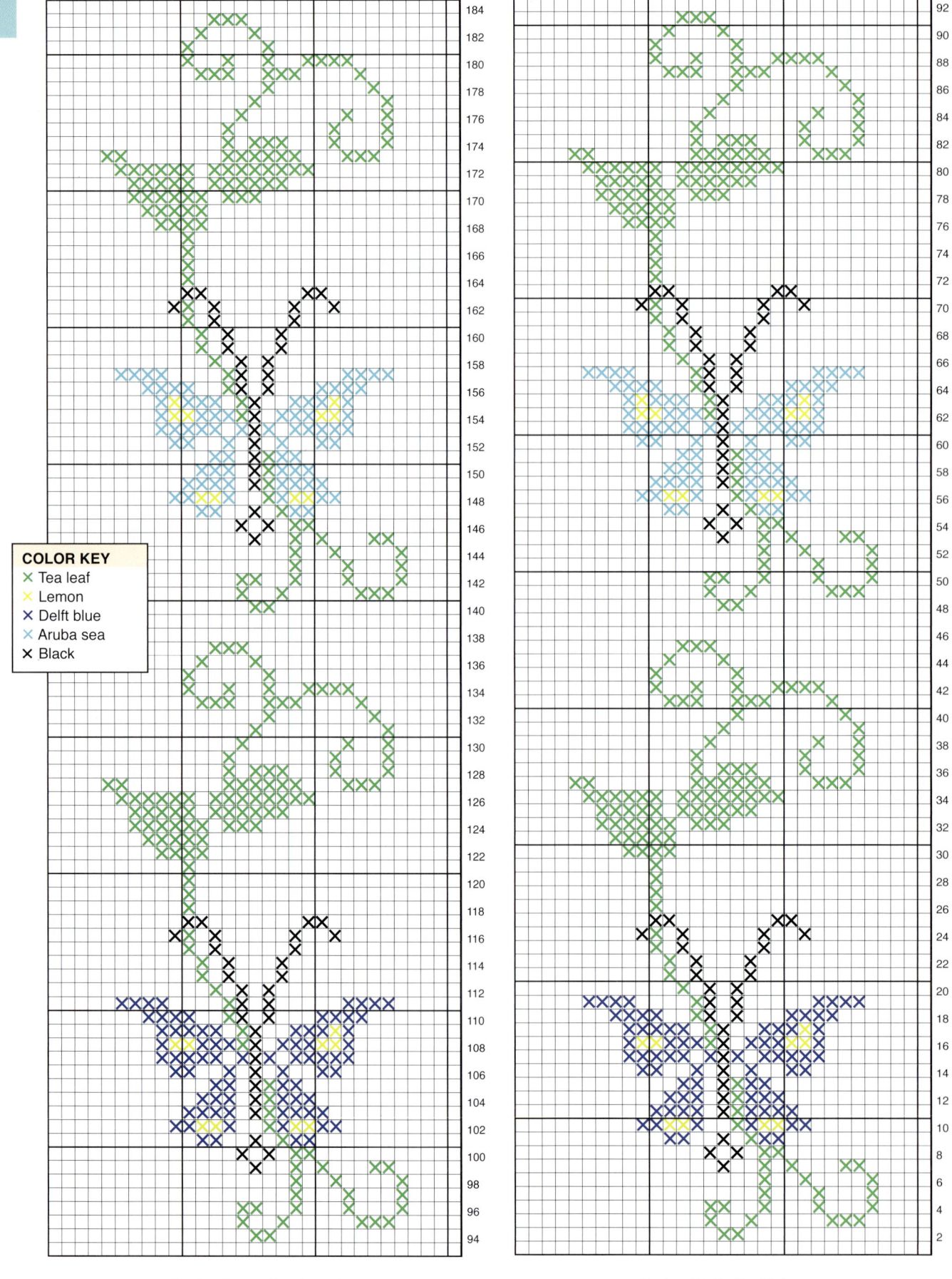

COLOR KEY
- × Tea leaf
- × Lemon
- × Delft blue
- × Aruba sea
- × Black

Spring Butterfly Afghan
Chart A Top of Panel

Spring Butterfly Afghan
Chart A Bottom of Panel

Spring Butterfly Afghan
Chart B Top of Panel

Spring Butterfly Afghan
Chart B Bottom of Panel

STITCH GUIDE

FOR MORE COMPLETE INFORMATION, VISIT ANNIESCATALOG.COM/STITCHGUIDE

STITCH ABBREVIATIONS

beg	begin/begins/beginning
bpdc	back post double crochet
bpsc	back post single crochet
bptr	back post treble crochet
CC	contrasting color
ch(s)	chain(s)
ch-	refers to chain or space previously made (i.e., ch-1 space)
ch sp(s)	chain space(s)
cl(s)	cluster(s)
cm	centimeter(s)
dc	double crochet (singular/plural)
dc dec	double crochet 2 or more stitches together, as indicated
dec	decrease/decreases/decreasing
dtr	double treble crochet
ext	extended
fpdc	front post double crochet
fpsc	front post single crochet
fptr	front post treble crochet
g	gram(s)
hdc	half double crochet
hdc dec	half double crochet 2 or more stitches together, as indicated
inc	increase/increases/increasing
lp(s)	loop(s)
MC	main color
mm	millimeter(s)
oz	ounce(s)
pc	popcorn(s)
rem	remain/remains/remaining
rep(s)	repeat(s)
rnd(s)	round(s)
RS	right side
sc	single crochet (singular/plural)
sc dec	single crochet 2 or more stitches together, as indicated
sk	skip/skipped/skipping
sl st(s)	slip stitch(es)
sp(s)	space(s)/spaced
st(s)	stitch(es)
tog	together
tr	treble crochet
trtr	triple treble
WS	wrong side
yd(s)	yard(s)
yo	yarn over

YARN CONVERSION

OUNCES TO GRAMS	GRAMS TO OUNCES
1 — 28.4	25 — 7/8
2 — 56.7	40 — 1 2/3
3 — 85.0	50 — 1 3/4
4 — 113.4	100 — 3 1/2

UNITED STATES		UNITED KINGDOM
sl st (slip stitch)	=	sc (single crochet)
sc (single crochet)	=	dc (double crochet)
hdc (half double crochet)	=	htr (half treble crochet)
dc (double crochet)	=	tr (treble crochet)
tr (treble crochet)	=	dtr (double treble crochet)
dtr (double treble crochet)	=	ttr (triple treble crochet)
skip	=	miss

Single crochet decrease (sc dec): (Insert hook, yo, draw lp through) in each of the sts indicated, yo, draw through all lps on hook.

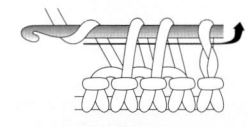

Example of 2-sc dec

Half double crochet decrease (hdc dec): (Yo, insert hook, yo, draw lp through) in each of the sts indicated, yo, draw through all lps on hook.

Example of 2-hdc dec

Reverse single crochet (reverse sc): Ch 1, sk first st, working from left to right, insert hook in next st from front to back, draw up lp on hook, yo and draw through both lps on hook.

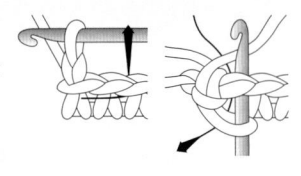

Chain (ch): Yo, pull through lp on hook.

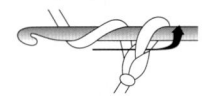

Single crochet (sc): Insert hook in st, yo, pull through st, yo, pull through both lps on hook.

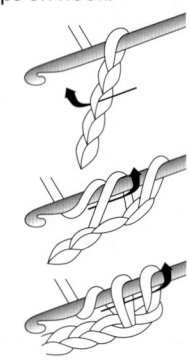

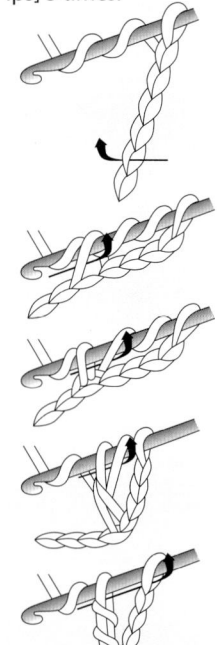

Double crochet (dc): Yo, insert hook in st, yo, pull through st, [yo, pull through 2 lps] twice.

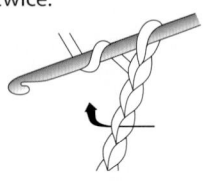

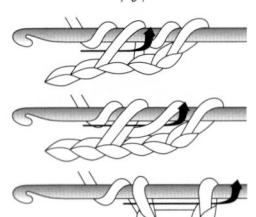

Double crochet decrease (dc dec): (Yo, insert hook, yo, draw lp through, yo, draw through 2 lps on hook) in each of the sts indicated, yo, draw through all lps on hook.

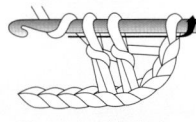

Example of 2-dc dec

Front loop (front lp) Back loop (back lp)

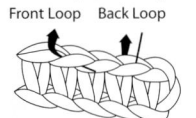

Front Loop   Back Loop

Front post stitch (fp): Back post stitch (bp): When working post st, insert hook from right to left around post of st on previous row.

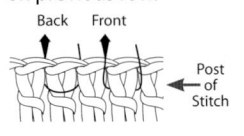

Back   Front
Post of Stitch

Half double crochet (hdc): Yo, insert hook in st, yo, pull through st, yo, pull through all 3 lps on hook.

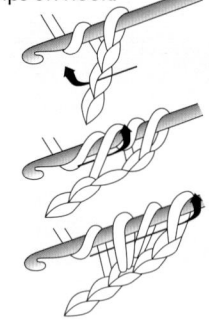

Double treble crochet (dtr): Yo 3 times, insert hook in st, yo, pull through st, [yo, pull through 2 lps] 4 times.

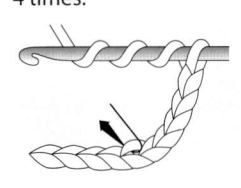

Treble crochet decrease (tr dec): Holding back last lp of each st, tr in each of the sts indicated, yo, pull through all lps on hook.

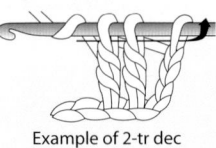

Example of 2-tr dec

Slip stitch (sl st): Insert hook in st, pull through both lps on hook.

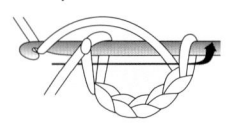

Chain color change (ch color change) Yo with new color, draw through last lp on hook.

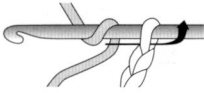

Double crochet color change (dc color change) Drop first color, yo with new color, draw through last 2 lps of st.

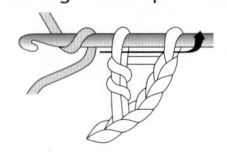

Treble crochet (tr): Yo twice, insert hook in st, yo, pull through st, [yo, pull through 2 lps] 3 times.

METRIC CONVERSION CHARTS

METRIC CONVERSIONS

yards	x	.9144	=	metres (m)
yards	x	91.44	=	centimetres (cm)
inches	x	2.54	=	centimetres (cm)
inches	x	25.40	=	millimetres (mm)
inches	x	.0254	=	metres (m)
centimetres	x	.3937	=	inches
metres	x	1.0936	=	yards

INCHES INTO MILLIMETRES & CENTIMETRES (Rounded off slightly)

inches	mm	cm	inches	cm	inches	cm	inches	cm
1/8	3	0.3	5	12.5	21	53.5	38	96.5
1/4	6	0.6	5 1/2	14	22	56	39	99
3/8	10	1	6	15	23	58.5	40	101.5
1/2	13	1.3	7	18	24	61	41	104
5/8	15	1.5	8	20.5	25	63.5	42	106.5
3/4	20	2	9	23	26	66	43	109
7/8	22	2.2	10	25.5	27	68.5	44	112
1	25	2.5	11	28	28	71	45	114.5
1 1/4	32	3.2	12	30.5	29	73.5	46	117
1 1/2	38	3.8	13	33	30	76	47	119.5
1 3/4	45	4.5	14	35.5	31	79	48	122
2	50	5	15	38	32	81.5	49	124.5
2 1/2	65	6.5	16	40.5	33	84	50	127
3	75	7.5	17	43	34	86.5		
3 1/2	90	9	18	46	35	89		
4	100	10	19	48.5	36	91.5		
4 1/2	115	11.5	20	51	37	94		

KNITTING NEEDLES CONVERSION CHART

Canada/U.S.	0	1	2	3	4	5	6	7	8	9	10	10½	11	13	15
Metric (mm)	2	2¼	2¾	3¼	3½	3¾	4	4½	5	5½	6	6½	8	9	10

CROCHET HOOKS CONVERSION CHART

Canada/U.S.	1/B	2/C	3/D	4/E	5/F	6/G	8/H	9/I	10/J	10½/K	N
Metric (mm)	2.25	2.75	3.25	3.5	3.75	4.25	5	5.5	6	6.5	9.0

Annie's® *Colorful Tunisian Afghans to Crochet* is published by Annie's, 306 East Parr Road, Berne, IN 46711. Printed in USA. Copyright © 2013 Annie's. All rights reserved. This publication may not be reproduced in part or in whole without written permission from the publisher.

RETAIL STORES: If you would like to carry this pattern book or any other Annie's publication, visit AnniesWSL.com.

Every effort has been made to ensure that the instructions in this pattern book are complete and accurate. We cannot, however, take responsibility for human error, typographical mistakes or variations in individual work. Please visit AnniesCustomerCare.com to check for pattern updates.

ISBN: 978-1-59635-927-7

1 2 3 4 5 6 7 8 9